W9-CNA-868

FORENSIC FILES

Investigating
Thefts & Heists

Heinemann Library
Chicago, Illinois

. . . . . ALEX WOOLF . . . . .

Originated by Ambassador Litho Ltd
Printed and bound in China by South China
Printing Company

08 07 06 05 04
10 9 8 7 6 5 4 3 2 1

**Library of Congress Cataloging-in-
Publication Data**
Woolf, Alex, 1964–
    Investigating thefts and heists / Alex Woolf.
        p. cm. -- (Forensic files)
Summary: Discusses some famous robbery cases
and describes how these
cases were solved using forensic science.
Includes bibliographical references and index.
    ISBN 1-4034-4833-7 (library bdg. : hardcover)
-- ISBN 1-4034-5473-6 (pbk.)
    1. Robbery investigation--Juvenile literature. 2.
Forensic
sciences--Juvenile literature. 3. Criminal
investigation--Juvenile
literature. [1. Forensic sciences. 2. Criminal
investigation.] I.
Title. II. Series.
    HV8079.R62W66 2003
    363.25'962--dc22

                                2003018159

Acknowledgments
The author and publisher are grateful to
the following for permission to reproduce
photographs:
pp. 4, 28 Rex Features; pp. 6, 19 Bob
Daemmrich/Topham/The Image Works; p. 8
Topham/Picturepoint; pp. 10, 20, 29, 30
Hulton Archive; pp. 11, 15 Katz; p. 13 David
Lassman/Topham/The Image Works; p. 17 Shuji
Kobayashi/Getty Images; p. 22 The Wellcome
Trust; p. 24 Frank Spooner Pictures/Gamma
Liason; p. 25 Agilent Technologies UK Ltd;
p. 26 PA Photos; p. 27 Geoff Tompkinson/
Science Photo Library; p. 31 Simon Fraser/
Science Photo Library; p. 32 Debby Callahan;
p. 33 Gary Hochman/Nebraska ETV Network,
for the Wonderwise Science Learning Series;
p. 34 Science Photo Library; p. 36 Topham/
Photonews/Metropolitan Police; p. 37 Peter
Menzel/Science Photo Library; p. 38 Harcourt
Index; p. 39 Volker Steger, Peter Arnold Inc./
Science Photo Library; p. 40 David Taylor/Mirror
Syndication; p. 41 Pascal Goethegluck/Science
Photo Library; p. 42 Topham/PressNet.

Cover photograph of gemstones reproduced
with permission of Rick Gayle/Corbis.

Every effort has been made to contact copyright
holders of any material reproduced in this book.
Any omissions will be rectified in subsequent
printings if notice is given to the publisher.

Disclaimer
All Internet addresses (URLs) given in this
book were valid at the time of going to press.
However, due to the dynamic nature of the
Internet, some addresses may have changed, or
sites may have changed or ceased to exist since
publication. While the author and publisher
regret any inconvenience this may cause
readers, no responsibility for any such changes
can be accepted by either the author or the
publisher.

Some words appear in bold, **like
this.** You can find out what they
mean by looking in the glossary.

Contents

What Is Forensic Science?

Forensic science is any science used in the course of a criminal investigation. Its purpose is to provide scientific **evidence** for use in a court of law. Forensic science draws from a number of different subjects, including chemistry, biology, geology, **psychology,** and **social science.**

What do forensic scientists do?

In a typical criminal investigation, crime scene investigators will gather material evidence from a crime scene. Forensic scientists then examine this for evidence to assist in the investigation and the trial. Evidence can be anything from the body of a murder victim to the tire tracks of a getaway car. Forensic scientists do not spend all their time in laboratories and offices. They are also often called upon to attend crime scenes, and to give evidence in court as expert witnesses.

A forensic scientist uses a microscope to analyze samples collected from a crime scene.

Investigating thefts and heists

The investigation of thefts and **heists** can involve a range of different forensic skills. Fingerprints are often the best form of evidence to be found at theft scenes. Today's forensic scientists benefit from increasingly sophisticated methods of recovering fingerprints. In cases of armed robbery, forensic scientists with **expertise** in **ballistics** are often called upon. There is also a frequent demand for the forensic **analysis** of glass, **toolmarks,** blood, and clothing fibers in theft and heist investigations.

Investigator's toolbox

Forensic scientists who work on thefts and heists have many scientific techniques at their disposal. Here are just a few of them:

- Ballistics: every gun leaves its own unique traces at a crime scene—for example, in the **striation** on the discharged bullet. Scientists can carry out test firings using a suspected weapon, then compare the striation on the two bullets using a **comparison microscope.** The microscope allows both bullets to be seen at once through an eyepiece or on a screen.

- Fingerprints: every person has a unique set of fingerprints that remain unchanged throughout his or her life. This uniqueness makes fingerprints an ideal form of identification. Sweat, body oils, and dirt mix to leave fingerprints on smooth surfaces. Fingerprint experts use powders and chemicals to make the prints visible. Experts are also helped by computer enhancement techniques, where a computer is programmed to work out a complete fingerprint from fragments. By analyzing and comparing millions of fingerprints in its database, it can draw conclusions about how fingerprints are typically structured. A computer can use this information to estimate the pattern of the missing areas of an incomplete fingerprint.

- Physical evidence: a crime scene contains a great deal of physical evidence, such as soil, glass, skin, hair, and fibers—all of which can be analyzed for clues. For example, soil found on the bottom of a shoe can be examined for the **pollen** it contains, which can indicate where the shoe's owner has been.

A woman arrives home one Sunday evening after a weekend away. Even before she enters her house, she realizes something is wrong. There are splinters of glass on the sidewalk and an unfamiliar tire tread mark on the driveway. Her heart is beating fast as she turns her key in the lock and opens the front door. The hallway is a mess. Drawers have been overturned, and their contents spilled out onto the floor. In the corner of her living room, the familiar view of her wide-screen TV and DVD player has been replaced by an empty space. The stereo is also gone, crudely ripped from its wall socket. Her hand trembles as she reaches for the phone and dials 911.

Searching the house

The operator sends out a call to a nearby police unit, and within 30 minutes two uniformed police officers have arrived. They search the house, but the intruder has clearly left. There are signs of a forced entry in the first-floor bathroom, where the window has been smashed. The police do not move or touch anything. It is vital that **evidence** of the crime is not disturbed. One of the officers questions the woman about what was taken, while the other stands outside the house to ward off any curious passers-by.

Gathering evidence

The crime scene investigator arrives next. Her job is to use scientific methods to help identify the burglar.

A crime scene contains a great deal of physical evidence, such as glass, hair, and fibers, which can be examined for clues.

Her first concern is to **preserve** the evidence. A plastic sheet is placed over the tire mark in the driveway for protection. Any surfaces that may have been touched by the burglar are dusted for fingerprints. The point of entry (the place where the burglar entered) is searched for footwear impressions, or marks made by tools to pry open the window.

In the midst of this activity, something catches the investigator's eye: a single strand of reddish hair lies on the shelf where the TV had once sat. Using a pair of tweezers she carefully places the hair in a transparent plastic bag. A clue has been found that could prove very useful in their efforts to catch the thief . . .

```
Crime scene procedure
When police are called to the scene of a burglary,
they carry out the following procedures:

• Approach the scene: assume the crime has just
  been committed, and be alert for any suspicious
  persons on approaching the scene.

• Secure the scene: ask the victim not to handle
  or move anything, and keep the victim in an
  undisturbed area of the house. Keep the number
  of people walking through the house as low
  as possible.

• Interview the victim: have the victim walk
  through the crime scene pointing out where
  any items are missing or have been disturbed.

• Look for evidence: the best evidence is usually
  found in the areas of greatest activity, and
  especially at the point of entry. Try to
  establish how and where entry was gained. Check
  doors and windows for signs of forced entry.
  Look for evidence such as footwear impressions,
  blood, and clothing fibers.
```

Forensic Science: the Early Days

The history of **forensic** science goes back to ancient times. Ancient Greek mathematician and inventor, Archimedes of Syracuse, employed science to discover the purity of the gold in the king's crown. He was able to prove that the king's goldsmiths, who had mixed the gold with common, inexpensive metals, had cheated the king. As early as the 700s, the Chinese recognized the value of fingerprints as a means of establishing identity.

Anthropometry

In the 1880s, Alphonse Bertillon, a French police employee, developed a theory that no two human beings could have identical physical dimensions. He used this **principle** to develop a system for identifying criminals. The system was known as anthropometry. It was based on measurements of the body such as length of feet, length of ears, and circumference of the head. However, anthropometry was soon overtaken by an even more precise technique: fingerprinting.

Fingerprints

The idea of using fingerprints to identify criminals was first proposed in 1880 by a Scottish doctor named Henry Faulds. In 1892, English scientist Francis Galton published *Fingerprints*, the first book to describe the unique

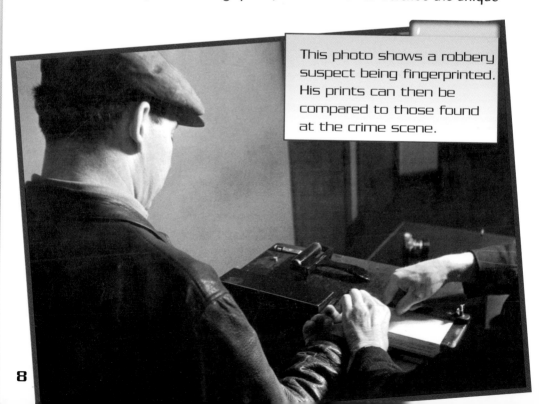

This photo shows a robbery suspect being fingerprinted. His prints can then be compared to those found at the crime scene.

and unchanging nature of fingerprints. This work influenced another Englishman, Sir Edward Henry, who in 1896 developed a classification system that would be used throughout Europe and the United States.

New methods

The 1900s brought further advances in forensics, including techniques for identifying blood, voices, faces, and trace **evidence** (evidence deposited in very small amounts at a crime scene), such as glass, fibers, and dyes. In 1900 Karl Landsteiner first discovered human blood groups. In 1910, Victor Balthazard published the first comprehensive study of hair, and three years later he published the first article to attempt to individualize bullet markings. In 1916, Albert Schneider invented a vacuum device to collect trace evidence, and in 1941, Murray Hill began to study voiceprint identification. Computers helped speed up investigations in the 1970s. In the 1980s came the first criminal convictions based on **DNA typing.** The **DNA** in our **cells** forms a pattern unique to each person, and it can be **extracted** from blood, tissue, and even flakes of skin, fingernails, and hair found at a crime scene.

Locard's exchange principle

In 1910, a professor of forensic medicine at the University of Lyon in France named Edmund Locard first stated his exchange principle. The principle purports that every contact leaves a trace. In other words, a criminal will always leave something behind at the scene of his crime that was not there before, and will always carry away something that was not on him when he arrived. For example, a burglar may cut himself while climbing through a window, leaving bloodstains on the windowsill. He may also carry away with him fragments of glass and paint embedded in his clothing.

This exchange principle forms the basis of forensic science.

On April 15, 1920, paymaster Frederick Parmenter delivered the $16,000 weekly payroll to a shoe factory in South Braintree, Massachusetts. He was accompanied by security guard Alessandro Berardelli, and, as always, both of them were alert for trouble. Even so, they failed to notice the two men loitering nearby. As Parmenter and Berardelli walked past them, one man suddenly pulled a gun from his pocket and fired at Berardelli, who was mortally wounded. Parmenter dropped his payroll bag and ran down the street, but he was chased by the gunman who shot him dead. The second man fired some more shots at Berardelli. Then the two men gathered the bags and jumped into a large black car that appeared from around the corner, and made their escape.

Anarchists accused

Police found four ejected .32 **caliber** cartridges near the bodies of Parmenter and Berardelli, manufactured by three firms, Peters, Winchester, and Remington. Eyewitnesses described the gunmen as Italian-looking, one with a large moustache, the other clean-shaven. On the night of May 5, two men fitting these descriptions were spotted in a streetcar in the area. The suspects, Nicola Sacco, a factory worker, and the mustachioed

Vanzetti (right) was identified as a participant in a previous bungled robbery at another shoe factory in nearby Bridgewater, Massachusetts.

Bartolomeo Vanzetti, a fish seller, were arrested. Both possessed loaded .32 caliber Colt pistols, and Sacco was carrying 23 bullets, all made by Peters, Winchester, and Remington. Their case was not helped by the fact that they were members of an extreme **anarchist** group supporting **revolution.**

"A witch-hunt"

The trial of Sacco and Vanzetti, held in Dedham, Massachusetts, began on May 31, 1921. A tense atmosphere surrounded the court. At this time the United States was in the grip of a "Red Scare," or fear of **communism.** Sacco and Vanzetti, with their radical beliefs, were considered to be dangerous **subversives.** The labor unions and communist groups that paid for Sacco and Vanzetti's legal defense called the trial a witch-hunt.

Striation analysis

Recovering the bullets from the crime scene was vital because they could help identify the gun used. The action of firing a bullet from a gun leaves marks known as **striations** on the cartridge. Striations are caused by the rifling—the spiral groove within the gun barrel that twists the bullet to give it a straight flight.

Every gun leaves unique striations. The technique of linking a bullet with a particular gun was first developed in 1898 by German chemist Paul Jeserich.

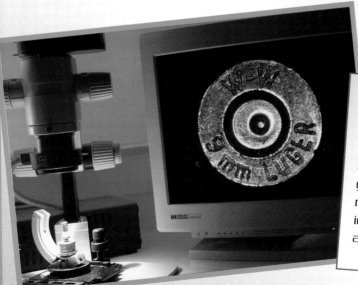

By 1922, there
vast database
striations and c
of all U.S. and
European makes
gun. The databa
made it easier to
identify the weap
a bullet came fro

Disputed evidence

The prosecution put forward 59 identification witnesses, and the defense put forward 99. So 99 people said Sacco and Vanzetti were not the killers, and 59 said they were. So much evidence presented to the court merely caused confusion, especially since many of the witnesses contradicted each other.

Ballistics testimony was equally inconclusive. Four bullets had been removed from Berardelli's body, and one from Parmenter's. The prosecution experts test-fired fourteen bullets from Sacco's gun into a box of oiled sawdust. The recovered bullets were compared to the fatal bullet taken from Berardelli's corpse. The **striations** were thought to be almost identical. A rust track at the bottom of the pistol barrel matched rust traces found on the fatal bullet. One prosecution expert concluded that Sacco's gun was definitely the murder weapon; the other only said it might be.

Old bullets

The defense experts, however, both insisted that Sacco's gun could not have fired the fatal bullets. But there was one aspect of the case that the defense had no answer to: the bullet that killed Berardelli was so old that another one could not be found to test Sacco's gun—except the equally old bullets found in Sacco's pockets. This **evidence** was enough to convince the jury, who returned a guilty verdict. Judge Webster Thayer sentenced the two men to death.

"Injustice"

The verdicts caused outrage around the world. The defense called for a retrial. They commissioned Albert Hamilton—who they later found out was a fraud who had falsely claimed **expertise** in firearms—to examine the bullet. Hamilton announced that the bullet had most certainly not come from Sacco's gun.

New evidence

In 1923, prosecution ballistics expert Charles Van Amburgh used enlarged photographs to compare the fatal bullet with bullets fired from Sacco's gun. He concluded that the striations were identical. Hamilton, worried that this evidence would prove him wrong, sneaked a new gun into court, and tried to switch the barrel of the new gun with the barrel on Sacco's gun while no one was looking. Fortunately, Judge Thayer saw him, and ordered him to hand over the real barrel.

Guilty as charged

The **controversy** raged on until 1927, when a committee was set up to review the case. It called upon the services of Calvin Goddard at the Bureau of **Forensic** Ballistics in New York. In the presence of a defense witness, Goddard fired a bullet from Sacco's gun into cotton wool, and then placed it beside the fatal bullet under a **comparison microscope.** It was clear that both bullets were identical.

The results were so convincing that even the defense expert was forced to agree with the conclusion: the fatal bullet had definitely been fired from Sacco's gun. Sacco and Vanzetti's guilt was confirmed and on August 23, 1927, despite worldwide protests, they went to the electric chair.

This detective uses a comparison microscope to try to find a match between the striations on two different bullets.

13

One night in September 1920, a thief used a saw to break into a grocery store in Berkeley, California. He helped himself to some cookies and a bottle of milk and departed. This minor offense marked the beginning of one of the strangest crime sprees in Californian history. Police investigating the case came across a fingerprint at the crime scene shaped like a question mark. No match could be found for this unusual print at Berkeley Police Department's recently established fingerprint bureau.

A creature of habit

Two weeks later there was another break-in—this time at a hardware store. The same method of entry was used, the identical question-mark print was found, and once again the burglar interrupted his activities to drink a bottle of milk. Throughout the winter the petty burglaries continued, following the same pattern, and always occurred between 9 P.M. and 4 A.M. In April 1921, the robberies suddenly stopped, only to start up again the following September. The burglaries stopped again in April 1922, and began again in September 1922. And so the pattern continued for the next six years.

Inspiration

By 1928, the burglar was stealing items worth thousands of dollars each. Police concluded that the burglar was probably a carpenter or plumber, because of the careful way in which he broke into properties. But where did such people go between April and September? In a moment of inspiration, Berkeley's police chief, August Vollmer, realized that skilled tradesmen would be needed for on-going maintenance on the fishing boats that went from Berkeley to the salmon fishing grounds in Alaska each summer.

The ship's carpenter

The police asked the fishing-boat company for the details of the expert workers they used. Thirty-eight names and addresses were sent, and these were forwarded to the Federal Bureau of Investigation (**FBI**), which deals with interstate crime. The FBI checked the set of names against their

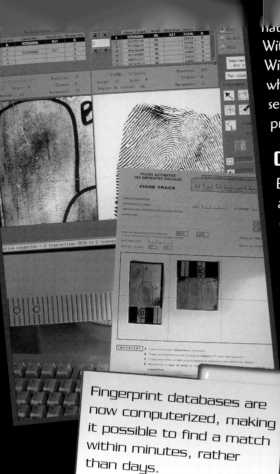

national register of fingerprints. Within days they had their man: William Berger, a ship's carpenter, who had been fingerprinted while serving time at San Quentin prison in 1914.

Caught

Berger's house was watched, and in September 1928 he was caught red-handed returning from a robbery. In the chase that followed he was shot dead. When his fingerprints were taken at the morgue, the distinctive question-mark print was found on the middle finger of his left hand. On searching his house, police found every item he had ever stolen—the proceeds of an estimated 400 thefts.

Fingerprint databases are now computerized, making it possible to find a match within minutes, rather than days.

National fingerprint database

When the question-mark burglar first struck in 1920, there was no national database of fingerprints in the United States. Criminals could commit crimes in different states knowing they would not be caught by their fingerprints. By 1924, the FBI had accumulated a database of 810,000 sets of fingerprints. These prints formed the core of what grew into a national system. By 1997, the FBI had more than 200 million fingerprints, representing 32 million people, on file.

The Preserved Body

David Paul was a 60-year-old delivery man for the Broadway Trust Bank in Camden, New Jersey. Each week he would carry a deposit to the Girard Trust Company in Philadelphia. On October 5, 1920, he left the bank as usual with a bag containing $40,000 in cash. But he never completed the journey. Eleven days later his body was found in a shallow grave near a stream in Burlington County. He had been shot twice and his skull was badly fractured. His clothing was soaking wet, which was odd because the ground around him was completely dry. The money was gone.

Big spenders

The **medical examiner** declared that Paul had died no more than 24 hours before the body was discovered. A pair of glasses were found near his body. The glasses were traced to a neighbor of Paul's named Frank James. According to locals, James and another man, Raymond Schuck, had been spending large amounts of money in recent weeks. When the two men were questioned, they both had airtight **alibis** for the time when the murder was thought to have taken place.

Tannic acid

Upstream from the place where Paul's body was found were a number of **tanning** factories. Tests on the water from the stream showed that it contained unusually high amounts of tannic acid, enough to act as a preservative on a human body. This alerted the police's suspicions. If Paul's body had been in the stream after he died, the tannic acid may have caused the medical examiner to underestimate the time that had passed since Paul's death.

Confession

When the police confronted James and Schuck with this new **evidence,** James immediately confessed to the robbery and murder. They had dumped Paul's body under a bridge where it had lain for several days partially underwater. Later they had retrieved the body and buried it in the shallow grave. Both men were found guilty of murder, and were sentenced to death.

Time of death

When a body dies it changes in several ways, and these changes can be measured in order to figure out when death occurred. The three principal indicators used to determine time of death are:

1. **Rigor mortis:** a progressive stiffening of a body begins about three hours after death, and continues for twelve hours. The process usually reverses after 36 hours, until a body is soft again.

2. **Lividity:** over a period of seven to eleven hours after a person dies, the red blood **cells** settle, causing the skin to turn red on the areas closest to the ground.

3. Body temperature: after death, a body is no longer taking in oxygen, which maintains the body's normal temperature. So the temperature drops at a rate of about one degree per hour.

None of these indicators are foolproof, and all three of these effects can be accelerated or slowed down by factors such as surrounding temperature, the build and health of a person, or the presence of alcohol or drugs.

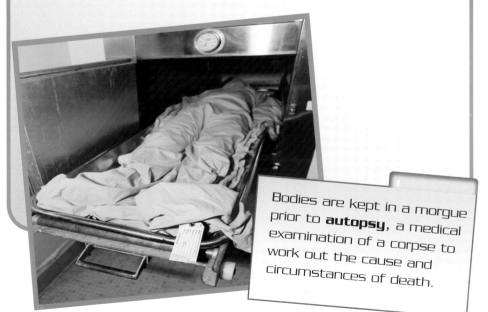

Bodies are kept in a morgue prior to **autopsy**, a medical examination of a corpse to work out the cause and circumstances of death.

On March 16, 1960, the bodies of three women bound with twine were found in a cave in Starved Rock Park in Utica, Illinois. The women, whose names were Lillian Oetting, Mildred Lindquist, and Frances Murphy, were all married to wealthy Chicago businessmen. The women had been robbed of their money and jewelry. **Autopsies** showed that they all died from skull fractures and brain damage. Near the cave, the murder weapon was found: a three-foot-long branch covered in blood.

Under suspicion

The police investigation focused on the employees and guests at the Starved Rock Park Lodge, where the women had been staying. Fellow employees remembered seeing scratches on the face of a dishwasher in the lodge on the day of the murders. This man, 21-year-old Chester Weger, became the prime suspect. When questioned about the scratches, Weger claimed he had cut himself while shaving. Police searched his home and found a bloodstained leather jacket, which they sent to the local police laboratory for **analysis.** Weger was given two **polygraph,** or lie-detector, tests. The results of both tests indicated he was telling the truth when he denied murdering the women. According to the laboratory report, the stain on the jacket was animal blood. Weger was in the clear.

The same twine

Then, in a tool shed at the lodge, they found pieces of the same twine that was used to tie the women up. The twine in the lodge had knots in it identical to knots found in the twine used to bind the murder victims. Among the few who used the tool shed was Chester Weger, who once again became the prime suspect. Weger's jacket was sent to the **FBI** Crime Laboratory in Washington, D.C. There it was revealed that the jacket stain was human blood after all, and from the same blood type as one of the murder victims.

Confession

Weger was once again subjected to a polygraph test, this time by polygraph expert, John Reid. The results showed that Weger was lying when he denied committing the murders. With **evidence** accumulating against him, Weger confessed. On March 3, 1961, he was sentenced to life imprisonment. Weger later admitted that he had fooled the polygraph machine on the first two occasions by swallowing aspirin with Coca-Cola, which calmed him down.

During a polygraph test, sensitive instruments record skin response, blood pressure. and respiration at the moment a question is asked.

Polygraph tests

A polygraph machine measures the **emotional responses** of people being interviewed, and reaches conclusions about whether or not they are telling the truth. The subject is asked two types of question: relevant questions (related to the crime) and control questions (calculated to provoke an emotional reaction). Innocent subjects are likely to react more to the control questions, and guilty subjects will react more to the relevant questions.

Sensitive instruments record skin response, blood pressure, and respiration (breathing). As the questions are asked, a connected stylus makes marks on a moving roll of paper. The examiner uses this to draw conclusions about how true the subject's answer was. Many psychologists claim that polygraph tests are unreliable because they cannot allow for people's different emotional responses. Evidence arising from polygraph tests is not always accepted in court.

FILE CLOSED

The Great Train Robbery

On the night of August 8, 1963, the "Up Special" Royal Mail train was making its regular run from Glasgow to London, England. In the High Value Package (HVP) car, Post Office staff were sorting valuable letters and packages into huge mail sacks. Just after 3 A.M., engineer Jack Mills saw a red signal ahead at Sears Crossing. In fact, the light had been deliberately changed from green to red by a gang of robbers. Mills could not know this, and he stopped the train. His co-engineer exited to find out what the problem was, but the track-side telephone lines had been cut. Before he could return to the train, he was attacked and thrown down the railway embankment. The Great Train Robbery had begun.

Unloading the loot

Another man climbed into the engine and clubbed Jack Mills over the head. He fell over unconscious. Jack Mills never fully recovered from his injury, and died in 1970. The armed robbers then forced the injured co-engineer to drive the train half a mile further to Bridego Bridge, where the rest of the fifteen-member gang was waiting. In the HVP car, the staff were forced into a corner while the robbers unloaded 120 sacks, containing £2.6 million (more than £30 million [$55 million] in today's money) in used banknotes. The whole robbery took just half an hour.

This is the scene of the Great Train Robbery in August 1963, with the train stopped at Bridego Bridge above a road where the other gang members were waiting.

Hideout

The gang then made their way to their hideout in Leatherslade Farm, Buckinghamshire. To pass the time, they played Monopoly—with real money! Meanwhile, a massive police operation was launched. The gang's hideout—by now abandoned—was located five days later. **Forensic** scientists took several days to examine the farm and the land immediately around it. They found fingerprints everywhere—on vehicles in the yard, windowsills, doors, crockery, beer cans, even on the famous Monopoly board. With this and other **evidence,** twelve of the fifteen robbers were caught, convicted, and jailed.

Lifting, examining, and matching fingerprints

Fingerprints are formed when the sweat and oils produced by the skin are deposited on a surface. On a hard, non-absorbent surface, a print is slightly raised from the surface. After a print has been dusted with powder to make it visible, it is removed from the surface with low-adhesive tape. Laser light or chemicals can be used to reveal prints on more porous surfaces such as paper.

Once sets of fingerprints have been obtained, they are magnified. The crucial features that make fingerprints unique are the broken ridges and bifurcations (points where lines divide). An examiner notes the relative positions of these features. A computer gives this information as a set of numbers and stores it in its database. This can then be compared to the sets of numbers of other prints already stored in the database in order to find a match. However, final identification is always made by a trained expert, not a computer.

One August night in 1967, thieves broke into a grocery store in a Scottish village and stole from the cash register. During the raid, an apple among the piles of produce tempted one of the robbers. He took a bite, and then finding it not to his taste, threw it away half eaten. The apple rolled under a store counter and was forgotten.

Plaster impression

The following day, police investigators discovered the apple and made a plaster impression of the bite mark. They had to work fast before the apple dried out and distorted the pattern of the teeth. Plaster was poured into the depressions made by the teeth. When the plaster dried, each impression was lifted out. Then the impressions were fixed together with wax to form a set of artificial teeth identical to those belonging to the thief.

Similar teeth

A few days later, two suspects were brought into the police station for questioning. One of the men had similar-looking teeth to the plaster-cast set. When a more detailed dental examination was carried out the teeth were found to be identical. Faced with this **evidence,** the man confessed, and the pair were found guilty of the theft. And the apple? It has been **preserved** in **formalin** and can be seen to this day with the bite mark still visible.

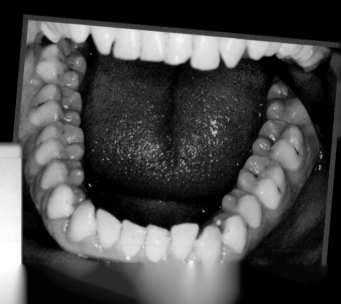

Generally, bite marks come from the front teeth in the upper and lower jaws.

Bite marks

Forensic dentists are often called upon to examine bite marks in food or on a victim's body. Bite marks can be very useful as a means of identification because each set of teeth has its own distinctive characteristics. These characteristics include size, shape, and relative position of teeth. They also include the alterations that occur through time, accident, or dentistry, such as wear and tear, restorations, fillings, loss of teeth, breakage, and injury. For this reason, teeth, like fingerprints, are unique.

Plaster casts of bite marks can be constructed to form an accurate copy of a set of teeth. Even this second-hand evidence can tell a forensic dentist a lot about the owner of the teeth, in some cases age, gender, and even racial origin.

- <u>Age:</u> the age of a person can be estimated by looking at the number of teeth fully erupted into the mouth, worn-down tooth surfaces (the older a person is the more worn-down their teeth become), the presence of wisdom teeth (which usually erupt between the ages of 17 and 25), or signs of their **extraction.**

- <u>Gender:</u> a person's gender can be worked out by looking at the size of the teeth. Men's teeth are generally larger than women's, especially the lower canine teeth.

- <u>Ethnic origin:</u> there are also dental features that are characteristic of different racial groups. For example, 95 percent of Native Americans and 91 percent of Chinese people have shovel-shaped incisor teeth That means they have flat, sharp-edged teeth in the front of the mouth used for cutting and tearing food.

Blowback

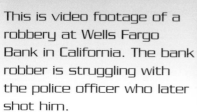

Michael Hart drove down the main street in Ham, Greater London, England. He parked his stolen car outside Barclays Bank, and checked his disguise in the rear-view mirror. He had darkened his skin with make-up, and was wearing sunglasses and a black wig. Concealed within his raincoat was a **sawed-off shotgun.** He got out of the car and calmly walked into the bank. Five minutes later a shot rang out, and Hart emerged with a bag containing £2,500 ($4,600) in cash, and made his escape.

This is video footage of a robbery at Wells Fargo Bank in California. The bank robber is struggling with the police officer who later shot him.

Shattered glass

Inside the bank, 20-year-old teller Angela Bullescroft lay behind her register, dead from a shotgun blast to her chest. The bullet had shattered the glass screen behind which Angela was sitting, causing tiny glass splinters, known as **spalling,** to fly outward. The splinters added greatly to her injuries.

Good detective work eventually led the police to Michael Hart. A search of his home uncovered much **evidence** of criminal activity, including a sawed-off shotgun, but nothing that could link him to the robbery at Barclays Bank. The police decided to recreate the shooting in a laboratory to see if it might yield them any clues.

Test firing

The police fired a shotgun through a glass screen from close range as Michael Hart would have done. They found that the spalling did not just fly forward towards the person sitting behind the screen, but also backward against the direction of the shot. This "blowback" would have embedded itself in Hart's clothing, and also in the barrels of the gun.

Making a match

The police re-examined Hart's shotgun and found particles of glass embedded in the barrels. Furthermore, they were able to match the particles to the spalling found in the bank. This evidence helped to convict Michael Hart, who was sentenced to life imprisonment.

Analyzing glass

Glass fragments can be compared because glass is **refractive**—light rays pass more slowly through glass than they do through space. The ratio between the speed of light through space and the speed of light through a piece of glass is called the **refractive index (RI).** Each type of glass has a different RI. Scientists can measure the RI of a glass fragment and compare it to the RI of fragments from another source in order to find a match.

To find the RI of a glass fragment, it is mounted in a drop of **silicone oil.** The RI of the oil changes according to its temperature. A halo appears around the fragment when its RI differs from that of the oil. The temperature of the oil is then raised or lowered until the halo disappears. The oil's RI is then calculated from a temperature/RI curve to give the RI of the glass.

Using special equipment, scientists can analyze even tiny fragments of glass.

In the early evening of November 11, 1974, 55-year-old Sidney Grayland was taking stock in the storeroom of his sub-post office in Langley, West Midlands, England. Hearing a noise he looked up to find himself confronted by a fit-looking man in combat fatigues, wearing a dark blue **balaclava.** The man, whose name was Donald Neilson, pointed a shotgun at Grayland, and demanded that he hand over the keys to the safe. Grayland refused, and leapt at Neilson, throwing him off balance. Before the thief could recover, Grayland reached for a can of household **ammonia** that he kept for just such an occasion, and sprayed it into Neilson's eyes. Neilson screamed in pain and pulled the trigger, shooting and killing Grayland. Temporarily blinded by the ammonia, Neilson fled from the scene.

Dark blue dye

Forensic scientists examining the scene at the sub-post office the following day found traces of a dark blue dye on the floor. Some of the ammonia sprayed in Neilson's eyes had evidently landed on the balaclava, causing the dye to leak out. They scraped up a sample for **analysis.**

Suspicious behavior

On the evening of December 11, 1975, Neilson was planning another robbery of a sub-post office in Mansfield, Nottinghamshire. Two police officers saw him acting suspiciously, as though he was planning a robbery, and stopped him for questioning. Neilson panicked and pulled out a shotgun. He forced them into his car. As they were driving, one of the officers grabbed the gun, which fired and blew a hole in the roof. After a struggle, Neilson was arrested.

Donald Neilson was sentenced to life imprisonment after being found guilty of murder.

Under interrogation, Neilson revealed his home address in Leeds. When searching his house, police discovered a dark blue balaclava. Forensic scientists were able to match the dye in this hat to the sample they had found on the sub-post office floor. This **evidence** helped link Neilson to the Langley robbery. His trial started on June 14, 1976, and Neilson—who had murdered a total of four people in the course of his five-year criminal career—was sentenced to life imprisonment.

Analyzing dyes

Dyes actually consist of a mixture of different colors. It is rare to find the identical combination of colors in two separate dyes, even if they look the same. To analyze a dye, the color **components** have to be separated out. This can be done by using a microspectrophotometer, a device that measures the amount of light that is absorbed through a transparent substance, such as a dye. Each color component absorbs light at a different rate. This rate can be displayed in a chart, giving an accurate picture of the dye's components, or using **thin-layer chromatography.** A sample of a dye is **extracted** in a **solvent** that is placed on a glass plate coated with a mineral named alumina. The components travel at different speeds along the glass plate due to differences in their **chemical composition,** and are thus able to be separated.

A scientist analyzes dyes with the help of a spectrometer, an instrument that uses **ultraviolet** or **infrared** light to work out the components of a dye.

Caught on Film

Charlie and Alec took the bus into the center of Glasgow, Scotland, and walked into the Clydesdale Bank. They approached the female teller, and Charlie carefully placed a gun on the counter. He kept his hand over it, so that only she could see it, and looked her in the eyes. "Do you see that?" he asked quietly. The woman nodded. Charlie pushed a bag under the glass screen. "Well would you fill that bag please." Under Charlie and Alec's watchful gaze, she placed all the money in her register into the bag, and passed it back to them. The two robbers then walked calmly out of the bank and made their getaway.

The publication of the Clydesdale Bank pictures was at first banned by a Scottish court because it was thought this might damage the suspects' chances of a fair trial.

The hold-up camera

A perfect robbery—except for one thing: Charlie and Alec had the misfortune of choosing one of the very first British banks to install a security camera. Some months earlier, security specialist John Mitchell had been on a trip to the United States, where 35-mm movie cameras, known as "hold-up cameras," had been installed above the exit doors of a number of banks. The cameras would be activated when a robbery took place. Mitchell was impressed by the technology, and persuaded the Clydesdale to install a camera in one of their branches. It just so happened that the branch chosen for this experiment was the very one Charlie and Alec had chosen to rob.

Legal controversy

The film of the robbery was processed and prints were made from the **sequence.** The quality was not good by today's standards, but it was good enough to be able to identify the robbers' faces. The bank and the police could publish the pictures in the hope that someone might recognize them and turn them in. But there was a problem: a Scottish court ruled that publication of the pictures might damage any suspects' chances of a fair trial. The police appealed against the decision, and eventually it was reversed.

In the papers

The pictures were published, and Charlie and Alec—by now hiding out in London, England—were shocked to see themselves in the newspapers. They felt safe in London, but when the proceeds of the **heist** ran out, they returned to Glasgow. Rather than continually live in fear of being recognized, the pair turned themselves in to the police. Charlie was sentenced to eight years in prison; Alec received five years.

Forensic photography

Photography has been used in police work ever since its invention. Between the 1850s and 1870s, many of the world's police forces began collecting photographic records of criminals to help with future identifications. Since the landmark case involving the Clydesdale Bank in Glasgow, photography is also used to catch thieves in the act.

Since then, security cameras have become standard in banks and building societies throughout the world. The picture quality of today's security cameras is far greater than was possible in the mid-1970s, and the **evidence** provided by these cameras has helped convict many thieves.

Camera-shy George Mason, a 19th-century bank robber, is held by four police officers as his picture is taken.

On the night of February 12, 1976, residents of a Hollywood apartment building were awakened by screaming: "Oh God, no! Help! Someone help!" This was followed by sounds of a struggle, and then silence. Seconds later a white man with long brown hair was spotted running from the scene, and then speeding away in a car. His victim was 37-year-old Sal Mineo, a former Hollywood star, who was found dying from a stab wound to the chest—a random victim of a brutal mugging.

Autopsy

Dr. Manuel Breton, Deputy **Medical Examiner** of Los Angeles County, carried out the **autopsy.** He **X-rayed** Mineo's lower chest and upper abdomen to see if they contained any metal fragments from the knife. He found none. Breton asked for the pierced section of Mineo's chest to be stored at the Los Angeles County **Forensic** Science Center, in case it might prove useful at a later date.

A lucky break

Sal Mineo was a popular actor in the late 1950s.

For two years the investigation failed to provide any significant leads. Then, in early 1978, Los Angeles police were told of a prisoner in Michigan named Lionel Williams who had bragged of stealing from and killing Mineo. When questioned Williams retracted his confession, but his wife confirmed that on the night of the murder he had come home covered in blood. Police uncovered further **evidence** linking him to a series of violent muggings around Los Angeles.

The weapon

There was just one problem. Every eyewitness claimed that the man running from the scene was white with long brown hair, whereas Williams was black with an Afro hairstyle. Leaving this awkward fact aside for the moment, police returned their attention to the stored chest section. Mrs. Williams had given police a good description of the hunting knife her husband had used for the attack. She even remembered the price—$5.28. With this was inserted into Mineo's chest wound, it matched perfectly.

An old photo

The case against Williams was looking very strong. The only thing left was the eyewitness accounts. It was shortly after this murder that a photo of Williams turned up in an old police file. It had been taken some years earlier when he had been under suspicion for another crime. It showed him with long hair, dyed light brown, and worn in a Caucasian style. Williams also happened to have light-colored skin, and it was easy to see how eyewitnesses might have mistaken him for a white man. Williams was found guilty and sentenced to life imprisonment.

Knife wound analysis

A forensic scientist will look at all aspects of a knife wound, including the depth of penetration, the direction and angle, and the probable force of the stabbing action. These factors may help create a picture of the circumstances of a death.

In the case of the Mineo stabbing, the knife wound was primarily examined with a view to discovering the type of weapon used. The wound was dissected surgically, layer by layer. The removed chest section was then placed in **formalin.** This process **preserved** it and made it firm, so that the blade of the knife could be inserted in the wound without fear of distorting its shape.

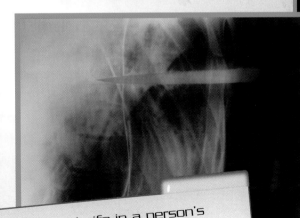

This colored X-ray showing a knife in a person's chest cavity. The shape of the wound can help identify the knife, like whether it had a single or double-edged blade, and whether it was sharp or blunt.

Mud Sticks

A store was robbed one night in a small New Zealand town. The thief escaped on a motorcycle, but not before the police were alerted. A police patrol car gave chase. The thief abandoned his motorcycle when it became stuck in the mud. He escaped by climbing up a muddy hillside. Several days later a man reported the theft of his motorcycle at the local police station. The bike matched the description of the one the thief had abandoned, and the night he claimed it was stolen was the night of the robbery.

Muddy boots

Police were suspicious because the man looked to be about the same size and build as the suspect. They asked him about his whereabouts on the night in question. He denied he had been in the area where the motorcycle was abandoned or on the nearby muddy hillside where the suspect had escaped on foot. On searching the man's house, police found a pair of muddy boots. Their owner claimed that the mud came from the farm where he worked.

Soil samples examined

A sample of the mud from the boots was sent to a **forensic** laboratory for **analysis,** along with soil samples collected from the hillside where the motorcycle was abandoned, and from the farm where the man worked. These samples were examined by a forensic palynologist (**pollen** specialist).

Pollen match

The types of pollen recovered from the mud on the boots closely matched the pollen recovered from the mud on the hillside, but were quite different from the pollen in the soil samples from the farm. This **evidence** was sufficient to prove in court that the farmworker was guilty of carrying out the store robbery.

Pollen found in soil samples collected from a pair of boots can help connect a suspect to a crime.

Forensic palynology

The study of pollen in the investigation of crime is called forensic palynology. Pollen is the powdery substance produced by flowering plants that fertilizes other plants. All soil contains pollen, and each **species** of plant produces its own unique type of pollen. Characteristics of pollen include its shape, size, weight, dispersal distance, durability, abundance, and "sinking speed" (the rate at which it falls to earth). By measuring these things a palynologist can determine what species of pollen it is.

A palynologist can usually determine the geographical source of a soil sample based on the type of pollen it contains. Samples of dirt collected from the clothing, skin, shoes, or car of a suspect may prove helpful in linking the suspect to a crime.

The **extraction** of pollen from the soil is done by means of a chemical reaction such as acetolysis (caused by mixing acetic acid with the soil sample) in order to dissolve or destroy all the non-pollen material. The pollen can then be analyzed under a microscope.

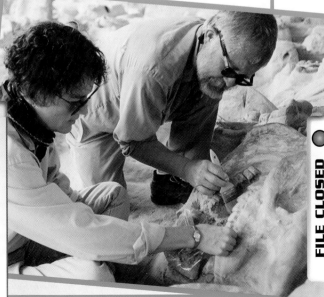

Strict procedures must be followed to avoid contaminating soil under examination. Samples are usually collected using a soft, clean brush and placed in sterile, self-sealing bags.

FILE CLOSED

In April 1996 a gang of armed robbers walked into a bank in Spokane, Washington, and demanded all the money in the cash box. The **heist** went smoothly and the gang escaped with thousands of dollars in cash. It was just one operation in a whole string of robberies and bombings that the gang would carry out in Spokane during the spring and summer of that year. The gang always wore masks to foil security cameras. It did not occur to them that they had left a vital clue to their identity—their jeans!

Search

In the late summer **FBI** agents arrested the suspects, and obtained a search warrant to search their homes and cars. Hundreds of articles of clothing, including 27 pairs of jeans, were taken in the search. The clothing was taken to look for traces of gunpowder that could link the gang to the bombings and to look for two particular pairs of denim pants.

Making a match

It so happened that the bank the gang robbed back in April had installed high-quality 35 mm security cameras.

A researcher at a crime laboratory examines a pair of jeans for **evidence.**

One member of the gang had been standing still long enough for the camera to pick up part of his faded jeans in very good detail. **Forensic** scientists found that a certain pair of jeans obtained during the search had about 25 features in common with the pair of jeans in the tape of the robbery.

On another occasion during the same robbery, one of the gang members had his back to the camera. A circular bulge in the rear pocket of his jeans, caused by a tin of chewing tobacco that he had stored there, was captured on film. A pair of jeans was found among the retrieved items with the identical pattern marking the back pocket.

Controversial evidence

The use of jeans as a means of identification remains **controversial,** particularly when it relies on the quality of a photograph. During the gang's trial, an expert witness for the defense claimed that the identifying patterns were common to many jeans. He produced 34 pairs with similar patterns to the jeans of the accused. However, in each case the FBI was able to show how the jeans were different. The evidence of the jeans helped send the gang to prison.

Analyzing denim

The method used to compare patterns in denim is similar to that used when comparing fingerprints or tire treads; a forensic scientist will be looking for unique patterns. When jeans are manufactured they are pulled through a machine that makes an irregular series of bumps along the seams; the bumps are never the same twice. As jeans are washed, the dye gradually rubs off, exposing the white cotton along the seams. Because of the inconsistencies in the manufacturing process, the fading will be different for each pair of jeans, thus making them unique.

Carbon and Docherty

In June 2001 police were called to an address in South London, England, after neighbors raised the alarm. In the bedroom of the apartment they found the body of 54-year-old Michael Reaney. He had been assaulted, tied up, and gagged. The apartment was a mess, and several items had been stolen. The police checked recent calls made on Reaney's cell phone. One had been made to download ring tones to a woman named Selina Hall, the girlfriend of Francis Carbon, who was a suspect in a number of recent hold-ups and burglaries. Carbon became a suspect in the Reaney killing, and so did his regular partner in crime, Andrew Docherty.

South London robbers

Carbon and Docherty met in June 2000. Docherty was addicted to cocaine. To feed his habit they stole from taxi drivers, prostitutes, and elderly people, often using violence in the process. By early 2001, they had begun carrying out armed robberies on South London liquor stores.

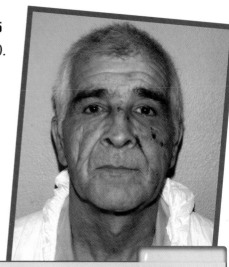

Following the Reaney killing, Carbon and Docherty were put under police **surveillance.** They were arrested while attempting to hold up a liquor store with an imitation handgun. Police searched their homes, as well as that of Bianca McCarthy, a business partner of Docherty's.

To feed his addiction to cocaine, Andrew Docherty and his partner, Francis Carbon, went on a prolonged crime spree in 2001.

A mass of evidence

As a result of the search, about 360 items were submitted for **forensic** examination. Tests on the items, carried out at the laboratories of the Forensic Science Service in London, established links between the suspects and the Reaney murder. For example, fibers on a pair of gloves at Carbon's home matched fibers found on the tape that had been used on Reaney's face.

Fiber analysis

To make a positive match between two fibers—for example from Carbon's glove and from the tape on Reaney's face—various tests are carried out. First, the color and physical appearance are compared using a **comparison microscope.** If the match appears good, the process is repeated using different types of light. Some colors appear the same in ordinary white light, but differences show up when viewed under **infrared** or **ultraviolet** light.

Natural fibers such as cotton and wool can be identified easily under a microscope. Cotton fibers are composed of concentric layers that enclose each other, while wool fibers are made up of overlapping scales like roof shingles. However, artificial fibers often appear the same, and a more complex test, **infrared spectrometry,** is used to tell them apart. Infrared spectrometry measures the amount of infrared light that is absorbed when it passes through a fiber. A chart is produced, showing peaks and troughs. This is called the fiber's signature, and it reveals the **chemical composition** of the fiber, which helps to identify it.

All fiber has its own unique structure.

At McCarthy's address, a pawn shop ticket was found. When their ticket was redeemed, police recovered three cameras and a pair of binoculars belonging to Michael Reaney. Film in the cameras was developed to show photos of Reaney at his home with McCarthy's son.

Blood match

Among the recovered items was a roll of black gaffer tape. Traces of blood were found on the inside of the roll. With a **DNA** test, it was possible to match this to the blood of one of the injured victims of a liquor store robbery. Blood found on Carbon's handgun, crash helmet, and tennis shoes was matched to two of the liquor store victims.

More evidence found

Minute traces of DNA were also found on a stereo remote control found in McCarthy's home. Unfortunately, the amount was too small to analyze by normal means. Instead, scientists turned to a recently developed method of **DNA typing** known as the DNA Low Copy Number method that allows tiny samples to be tested—up to ten times smaller than is required for traditional DNA typing.

Using this method, scientists found that the DNA on the remote control matched Reaney's DNA. Fingerprints on the same remote control were later identified as Carbon's and Docherty's. Yet another link was established between the suspects and their victim.

Film from three cameras belonging to the victim, Michael Reaney, was developed to show photos of him with associates of Andrew Docherty.

Dog hairs

A number of animal hairs were found on the ropes used to bind Reaney. The hairs were sent for testing to see if they matched the hairs recovered from the dog's bed at Carbon's home. The method used to match these hairs was **mitochondrial DNA** typing. This tests the DNA found in the mitochondria—the structures within a **cell** that produce its energy. Tests proved that the hairs from the ropes all came from the same dog, but the hairs found at Carbon's home came from a different dog. So this part of the **forensic** investigation failed to provide a link.

Sentenced

The huge amount of **evidence** provided by the forensic tests on the items found in the search was sufficient to convict Carbon and Docherty of a whole series of crimes. Carbon was jailed for eleven years, and Docherty received a fifteen-year sentence.

DNA Low Copy Number (LCN) profiling

DNA LCN is helping forensic scientists solve cases in which only tiny traces of DNA have been found, such as the human DNA found on a maggot that has been feeding on a corpse. This method increases the quantity of DNA to make it easier to sample through a process called polymerase chain reaction (PCR). The DNA sample is alternately heated and cooled alongside a substance called polymerase. This causes a **chain reaction** that copies the DNA fragment many times until it is big enough to be analyzed. The method takes several weeks—much longer than traditional DNA typing.

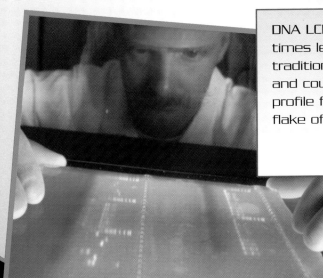

DNA LCN requires ten times less DNA than traditional methods, and could produce a profile from a single flake of dandruff.

The Carjacking Mob

One night in late March 2002, a gang of men stopped their car outside a house in North London, attracted by the sight of the BMW in the driveway. They donned their ski masks and approached the house. One member of the gang, Leon Willoughby, was casually eating a kebab. The gangsters kicked in the front door and confronted the terrified family. One gang member pulled out a gun and demanded the keys to the car. The car's owner went to look for them. While they waited for his return, Willoughby wandered over to the back of the house. He tossed the remains of his kebab out of the window into the garden. Minutes later the gang made their escape in their new BMW.

Several of the carjackers posed as 1920s Chicago gangsters in this photo that was later used as **evidence** against them.

High-speed chase

Between February 20 and March 26, 2002, this seven-man gang of violent carjackers terrorized parts of North London. Their luck ran out on the night they stole the BMW. As they sped along the highway at 120 mph, they were pursued by police and arrested. Police then uncovered the extent of their 35-day crime spree: nineteen cars worth a total of £350,000 ($643,240) had been stolen in 28 raids.

Clues in the kebab

In court, the gang's guilt was established by good **forensic** work. Crime scene investigators found the remains of Willoughby's kebab at the scene of their final raid. Scientists linked traces of saliva found on the kebab to Willoughby through **DNA typing.**

DNA is a kind of **molecule** found in the **cells** of all living creatures. Our DNA determines our physical characteristics, and it is what makes us unique—that is why it is useful for determining identity. Scientists can examine DNA **extracted** from blood, hair, skin tissue, or saliva. The DNA extracted from the saliva on the kebab was compared to Willoughby's DNA, and they were found to match. The carjacking gangsters were found guilty and sentenced to between nine and fourteen years in prison.

This X-ray photograph of bands of DNA is being studied.

DNA typing

DNA is made up of four chemicals that are strung together in long **sequences.** A sample of DNA is mixed with a substance that cuts the DNA chain at particular sequences. The fragments are placed in a gel and an electric current is applied. Shorter fragments move more quickly through the gel than longer fragments, and they line up according to size. Special **radioactive** sequences of DNA are then added, which stick to the other sequences. Because they are radioactive, an **X-ray** photograph reveals the pieces of DNA as dark bands. This "DNA fingerprint" can be compared to DNA sequences from other specimens to find a match.

So you have read the book. You have seen the professionals in action. Now solve a crime for yourself. Imagine that you are a **forensic** scientist. You must decide which of the techniques described in the book you would use to solve the following case.

The aftermath

The security van was a wreck. Its front was flattened against the side of a large truck that was blocking the road. The reinforced metal doors at the van's rear had been smashed in. Shattered glass from the side window glittered on the road. Glass fragments had also cut the face and body of the driver who was sprawled lifelessly in his seat, a bullet wound visible at his temple.

The clues

Police taped off the scene in a side road off a busy shopping street while crime scene investigators searched the van and the body for clues. The security van had contained $2.8 million in cash, all of which had been taken.

The robbers had been careful to wear gloves and masks, so no fingerprints were found, and no witnesses could identify them. However, crime scene investigators found a few clues: on the tip of a jagged piece of metal—part of one of the smashed rear doors—was a piece of skin and a shred of fabric. These, plus samples of the smashed glass and the bullet retrieved from the driver's body, were handed to forensic scientists at the crime lab

Police believed that this was the latest in a string of robberies being committed by a gang operating in the area. The suspects' homes were searched, and a number of items were retrieved, including three firearms and several items of clothing. On the morning of the robbery, some members of the gang had been seen by witnesses. There was only one period, between 10:30 and 11:15 A.M., when the gang's movements were unaccounted for.

What you must do

You are a forensic scientist working at the police crime laboratory. How would you go about the following tasks?:

1. Establish the time of the robbery to see if it could have taken place during the period when the gang had no **alibi.**

2. Determine whether one of the guns found in the suspects' homes was used in the robbery.

3. Find any other links between the suspects and the security van robbery.

ANSWERS:

1. The medical **examiner** assigned to the case will be able to estimate the time of death based on **rigor mortis, livitity,** and body temperature. This will give you the approximate time of the robbery.

2. Test fire the guns found in the search and compare the **striations** to those found on the bullet retrieved from the driver's body to see if there is a match. Another possible way of matching the gun to the crime is to check for any **spalling** that may have become embedded in the gun's barrel from the shattered window. The **refractive index** of the samples from both sources can be compared.

3. The fibers in the shred of fabric can be compared to fibers in the items of clothing found in the search using **infrared spectrometry.** The dyes in the fibers can be compared using **thin-layer chromatography. DNA** tests can be carried out on the skin to see if it matches any of the suspects.

Glossary

alibi claim that a suspect was elsewhere at the time that a crime was committed; proof of such a claim

ammonia colorless gas with a pungent odor

analysis detailed examination of something in order to understand it better

anarchist person who rejects the need for a formal system of government

autopsy medical examination of a corpse to determine the cause and circumstances of death

balaclava knit covering for the head and neck, leaving only the face, or parts of it, exposed

ballistics study of firearms and ammunition

caliber inner diameter of the barrel of a firearm

cell smallest independent unit in an organism

chain reaction series of events one after the other, each of which causes the next one

chemical composition atoms and molecules that make up a substance

communism system in which the state controls wealth and property

comparison microscope microscope that allows the viewer to see two objects at the same time for purposes of comparison

component part of something, usually of something bigger

controversy disagreement on a topic that causes strong feelings

DNA type of molecule in the form of a twisted double strand (known as a double helix) found in every cell of every living thing. DNA is a major component of chromosomes (the rod-shaped structures in a cell nucleus) and carries genetic information (the information that determines an organism's characteristics).

DNA typing forensic method of identifying a person by analyzing their DNA

emotional response reaction that involves feelings

evidence something that gives a sign or proof of the existence of something

expertise skill or knowledge of someone who knows a lot about a particular subject

extract obtain something from a source, usually by separating it out from other material

FBI Federal Bureau of Investigation; a bureau of the U.S. Department of Justice that deals with matters of national security, interstate crime, and crimes against the government

forensic relating to the application of science in the course of a criminal investigation

formalin solution of formaldehyde (a colorless gas) in water, used for preserving organic specimens

heist   slang term for an armed theft or robbery

infrared   portion of the electromagnetic spectrum (the complete range of radiation), invisible to the human eye, consisting of radiation with wavelengths between light and radio waves

infrared spectrometry   method used to measure the degree to which infrared light is absorbed when passing through a transparent substance. This measurement, called a "signature," can be compared to the signatures of other known substances as a way of identifying the unknown substance.

lividity   process in which red blood cells in a corpse settle shortly after death, causing changes to the body's skin color

medical examiner   doctor appointed to establish the cause of someone's death, especially in cases where death is not from natural causes

mitochondrial DNA   form of DNA found in the mitochondria—the structures that produce a cell's energy. Mitochondrial DNA is harder to test than ordinary DNA and can only indicate relationships through the maternal line. However, because it is less fragile than DNA from a cell nucleus, it can be found in very old remains and provides important information about archaeological finds.

molecule   two or more atoms held together by chemical forces

pollen   powdery substance produced by flowering plants. It is carried by wind and insects to other plants, which it fertilizes.

polygraph   electric device that measures involuntary physical activities, such as pulse rate and perspiration. It is often used as a lie detector.

preserve   keep something protected from anything that might cause it to deteriorate

principle   important law or assumption that is used as a basis for a system of thought

psychology   study of the human mind and human behavior

radioactive   energy as a stream of particles formed by the decaying of unstable atoms

refractive   describing a substance that refracts, or causes light to change direction when it passes through it

refractive index (RI)   ratio between the speed light travels through a vacuum and the speed light travels through a piece of glass

revolution   violent overthrow of a ruler or political system

rigor mortis   progressive stiffening of the body that occurs several hours after death

sawed-off shotgun shotgun with the end of the barrel sawed off to mute the sound it makes when fired. A shotgun is a short-range, shoulder weapon that fires small pellets.

sequence section of a motion picture showing a single incident; a set of related actions or events.

silicone oil silicon-based oil used as an insulator or water repellent

social science study of people in society and how individuals relate to one another and to a group

solvent substance in which other substances are dissolved

spalling tiny fragments or splinters of glass, stone, or mineral

species group of animals or plants that are biologically similar

striation marking with parallel grooves or narrow bands

subversive person involved in activities intended to overthrow a government

surveillance continual observation of a person, especially one suspected of doing something illegal

tanning conversion of animal skins and hides into leather

thin-layer chromatography form of chromatography in which the components of a liquid are separated from each other. A sample of a liquid is extracted in a solvent, which is placed on a glass plate coated with a thin layer of a substance called alumina (colorless aluminum oxide). The components travel at different speeds along the glass plate because of differences in their chemical composition.

toolmark mark made by a tool—for example, a crowbar—in order to gain entry into a building or safe

ultraviolet portion of the electromagnetic spectrum (the complete range of radiation), consisting of radiation with wavelengths beyond the violet end of the visible light spectrum

X-ray high-energy electromagnetic radiation that is capable of penetrating solid objects

Get into Forensics

Forensics is a complex and fascinating business. Investigators may be called upon to make identifications from DNA fragments, take fingerprints from a crime scene, check photographs for fakes, examine paper fibers under an electron microscope, find the age of ancient bones using radiocarbon dating, match tire tracks left by a getaway car, or compare known dental records to the corpse of an unknown person.

One person alone cannot master such a wide range of skills, and those involved in forensic investigations often perform highly specialized tasks. Ballistics experts, for example, will match projectiles with weapons and detect traces of explosives on fabric or skin. Toxicologists may be called on by a pathologist carrying out an autopsy to examine a particular organ for indications of a hard-to-detect poison.

In their way of working, all forensic investigators are scientific or medical professionals. In fact, the range of skills required is so broad it covers almost every aspect of science and medicine: physics, chemistry, biology, medicine and dentistry, anthropology, archaeology, and psychology. So any reader wanting to pursue a career in forensics will need to begin with an interest in science.

Useful Websites

A website that gives details of the criminal mind and the methods they use:
http://www.crimelibrary.com/index.html

A site that gives detailed articles about various crime scene investigator techniques and tools:
http://www.crime-scene-investigator.net/

The FBI's website for young adults:
http://www.fbi.gov/kids/6th12th/6th12th.htm

Further Reading

Innes, Brian. *Forensic Science.* Broomall, Penn.: Mason Crest Publishers, 2002.

Pentland, Peter and Pennie Stoyles. *Forensic Science.* Broomall, Penn.: Chelsea House Publishers, 2003.

Woodford, Chris. *Criminal Investigation.* Chicago: Raintree, 2001.

FORENSIC FILES

Index